Meet the Beaver

Meet the Beaver

LEONARD LEE RUE III
with William Owen

Illustrated with photographs by Leonard Lee Rue III

G. P. PUTNAM'S SONS • NEW YORK

Published in 1989 by G.P. Putnam's Sons,
a Division of The Putnam & Grosset Group, New York.
Published simultaneously in Canada.
Printed in the United States of America.

Library of Congress Cataloging-in-Publication Data
Rue, Leonard Lee.
Meet the beaver/Leonard Lee Rue III with William Owen:
illustrated with photographs by Leonard Lee Rue III.
p. cm.
Reprint. Originally published: New York: Dodd, Mead, c1986.
Includes index.
Summary: Discusses the physical characteristics,
behavior, range, food habits, and enemies of one of the
few animals that purposely alters an environment
to fit its needs.
ISBN 0-399-61236-X
1. Beavers–Juvenile literature. [1. Beavers.] I. Owen.
William, 1942–. II. Title.
[QL 737.R632R84 1989] 599.32'32–dc 19 88-38298 CIP AC

10 9 8 7 6 5 4 3 2

To Barbara Dalton McMickle, who has been my secretary, my friend, and member of my family for many years. In appreciation of her efforts on my behalf—L.L.R.

To the Smith Colony: a hard-working, fun-loving, proud-nurturing family that has never given up and has altered the environment from coast to coast. It's good to be a part of you—W.O.

Contents

A large beaver

Preface

The beaver is an enormously interesting animal. It has always been important to man because it is one of the few animals that purposely alters an environment to fit its needs, and because of the popularity of its fur for the making of beaver hats.

Most animals will dig or build some sort of shelter, and perhaps their eating habits will occasionally change the landscape, such as overgrazing by moose. But only the beaver forms lakes and ponds for its own protection, for transportation, and for making it easier to obtain food and building materials for its home. In many ways, the beaver reminds me of mankind, and for this reason I have studied and photographed beavers extensively for over forty years. Before I put on scuba gear and went swimming with these creatures, no one had ever photographed them underwater. I discovered how they swim, and how they use their tails as rudders, and the special use of their front legs — not for swimming at all but held close to the chest to grasp food or mud or stones.

In order to photograph beavers where they live, one must be willing to invest many hours. A typical shooting schedule for beavers — which are mostly nocturnal — extends from dusk to dawn. This means getting to the location an hour before the sun sets and setting up cameras and equipment in a blind used for camouflage. If I am late and make a disturbance, the beavers will disappear.

One year in New Jersey I worked this way for one week out of every month during the full moon for months on end. This enabled me to see the animals by the light of the moon and focus before shooting them with a flash. Of course the flash would startle the beavers and I would have to wait as long as six hours for them to come back for another picture. This meant an entire night's investment for just two pictures! Yet the experience of encountering wildlife in their natural surroundings makes wildlife photography one of the most satisfying careers I know of.

I discovered that, like people, beavers form habits and are therefore predictable. One family of beavers I was photographing at Horseshoe Lake in Alaska kept a very strict schedule. They would enter and leave their lodge at precise times, providing they weren't disturbed or threatened by nosy photographers or predators. An older couple came hiking there one day and asked if it were possible to see beavers in this particular pond. "Of course," I replied. "The male will be coming out for dinner

Beaver towing a branch underwater

in exactly ten minutes. Just wait there on that bank and watch." I could tell by the queer looks that passed between them that they didn't believe me. They had no way of knowing that I had been living with these creatures for two weeks and knew their habits fairly well. The big male always came out of the lodge first to check danger, and he did this every afternoon between 4:15 and 4:30 P.M. At

4:20 P.M. on this day I saw the water swell some feet from the main lodge and then a wet, furry head popped above the surface of the pond. I turned to see the smile of approval from the couple as they looked over, pointing to the beaver.

I first trapped beavers for their fur when New Jersey opened the season on them after it had been closed for over one hundred years. I learned to trap during the Depression and the money I earned from animal pelts was my spending money. Today, although beaver fur is still valuable, I haven't trapped for years; I am more interested in the way of life of the beaver. I am continually amazed by their fascinating habits. They fell large trees, prune bushes, build dams, and dig canals. They mate for life, and most build permanent lodges in the middle of their ponds. I hope to be able to keep my eye on them for another forty years. And I hope you become as fascinated with these animals and become their friends as I have. Because of the pressure of our growing human population, and the shrinking acreage for wildlife, these and other animals are going to need all the human friends they can get.

1

Meet the Beaver

There isn't another mammal, with the exception of man, that alters its environment to suit its needs as does the beaver. It is famous for its dam-building abilities. The ponds that result go through evolutionary steps of open water, swamp, marsh, meadows, and back to forest again. If beavers build a dam in a wilderness area, they create an outdoor laboratory second to none. However, if they do their building on private land, they may flood pastures needed for grazing, destroy crops, fell valuable timber, destroy trout streams, block culverts, and even flood roads. The beaver is a boon or an abomination, according to whose trees are being cut down, whose land is being flooded, or whose river is dammed up.

Yet the diligent beaver has played an important role in the development of North America. Its dam-building activities resulted in the creation of much of our most fertile land. The beaver also prompted much of the early exploration and settlement of the continent. The early settlers soon learned that fortunes could be made in trading for beaver skins.

The beaver is a rodent, a member of the order of mammals known as Rodentia, characterized by front teeth adapted for gnawing and cheek teeth adapted for chewing. Nearly half of all mammal species are rodents. They include squirrels, groundhogs, chipmunks, as well as mice and rats, muskrats and guinea pigs. The beaver is the largest living rodent except for the capybara that inhabits Central and South America and gets to be four feet long and weighs 75 to 110 pounds.

The beaver has four incisor teeth in the front of its mouth, two on top and two on the bottom. The foreparts are bright orange in color. As with all rodents, these four teeth grow throughout the entire life of the animal. They must be kept worn down, but since these are the teeth used for gnawing, that is taken care of by beavers when cutting down trees and shrubs used in their building activities. Occasionally a rodent will suffer from what is called malocclusion, where the teeth do not oppose each other and are not worn down properly. The teeth continue to grow in an arc, eventually growing back and piercing the animal's skull. Or the teeth may prevent the animal from opening and closing its mouth, so that it starves. But these are rare cases. I've never seen this happen to a beaver, but I have found the skulls of woodchucks to whom this unfortunate accident has occurred.

An average adult beaver is three to four feet long,

A beaver's incisor teeth. These large front teeth used for gnawing are characteristic of all rodents.

including the tail, which is about 12 inches long and as much as 5 inches wide. A full-grown beaver weighs from 40 to 60 pounds and stands 8 to 9 inches at the shoulder, but the back is humped as high as 12 inches or more. For years the world record beaver was one taken by Vernon Bailey in 1921 on the Iron River in Wisconsin. It weighed 110 pounds. That record was broken by John Webster of Tie Siding in the Laramie Mountains of Wyoming. In

1938, Webster caught a beaver that weighed 115 pounds. Size is determined by age and the availability of food. A 90-pound beaver caught by Henry Mullins in Otterville, Missouri, in 1960 was 60 inches long — five feet.

The tail of the beaver is unique. It is a flattened appendage of cartilage and bone that is covered with scales. The platypus, an Australian mammal, also has a broad, flattened tail but it is covered with fur. The beaver's tail is naked and from 9 to 12 inches long, about ½ inch thick, and 3½ to 5 inches wide.

The scaley tail and webbed hind feet of a 55-pound beaver

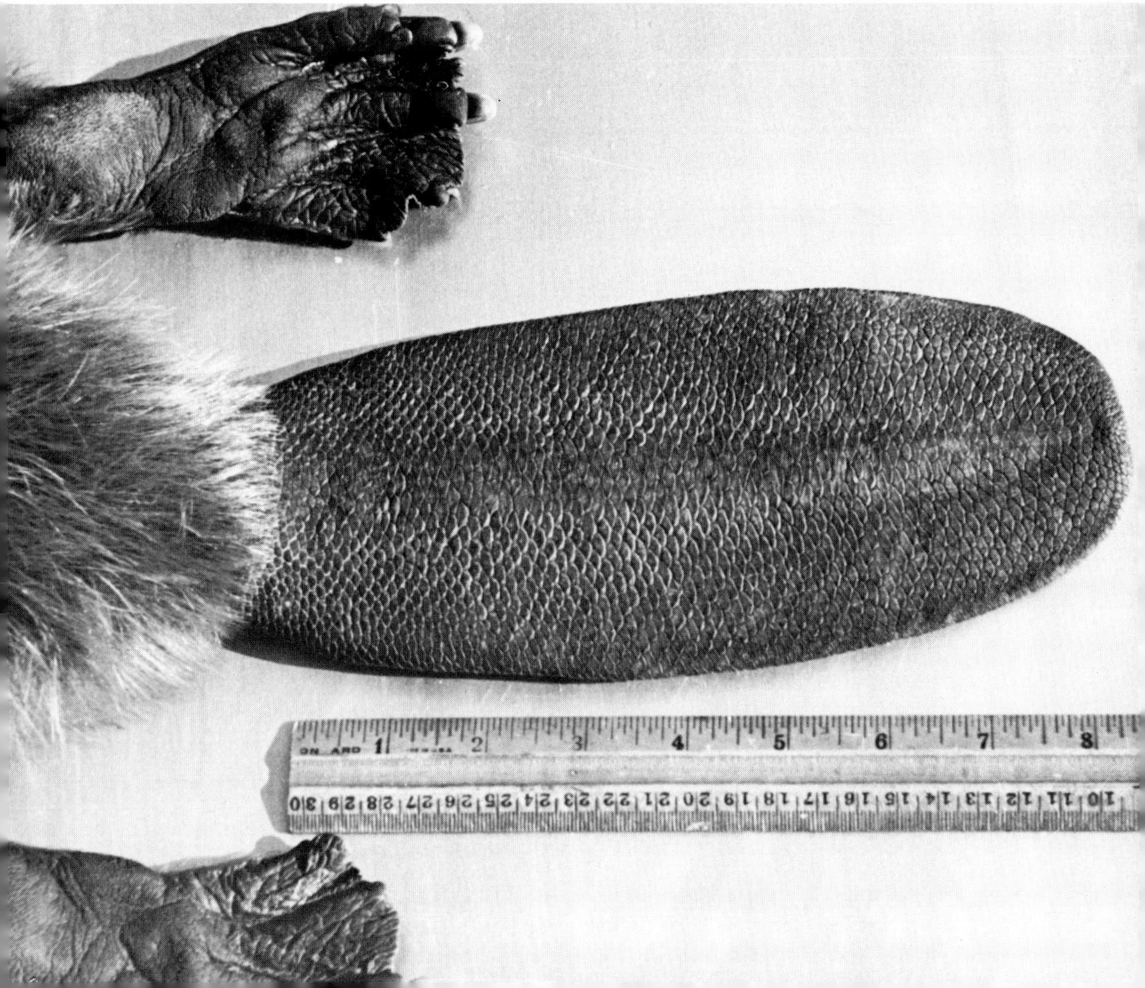

Of the many myths concerning the beaver, one is that it used its tail to pack mud on its dams. The tail of a beaver has many uses, but this is not one of them. A beaver uses its tail to slap the water as a warning signal of approaching danger. If a beaver was seen giving the signal near or on its dam or lodge, it could have been mistaken as part of its work. I've observed beavers for thousands of hours and have never seen them patting mud with their tails. The tail serves as a very effective prop when the animal sits upright to feed or is at work cutting down a tree. The tail is also used in swimming, but only for propulsion when the beaver is swimming very fast. It acts as a rudder, helping the beaver make turns or aiding in diving or surfacing.

The beaver is a semiaquatic mammal, spending time both on land and in the water. It depends on water for protection against enemies. It can swim in even the coldest weather and not freeze because of its body shape and its fur. Its large compact body has a relatively small surface area for its mass, which is very efficient for conserving body heat. Also, beneath the beaver's skin are a layer of tough tissue and a layer of fat that provide excellent insulation.

The beaver's fur, when properly groomed with oil from its own oil glands, is literally waterproof. The skin stays dry and hence warmer.

Beavers have long been famous for their fur. It is valued for making fur coats. If you've never seen a live beaver, you might not recognize the difference between a beaver fur coat and the fur on the live animal. This is due to the long guard hairs on the beaver's pelt. About two inches in length, they overlay the soft, dense undercoat of hairs that are a little less than an inch in length. These guard hairs are usually plucked or cut before the fur is used to make a coat.

Beaver fur ranges in color from light reddish brown to nearly black. The darker pelts have the greater value and come from the northern areas, while the lighter animals are found farther south. Most beavers appear to be dark brown with reddish guard hairs. Occasionally, white albinos occur, although I've never seen one.

In keeping with its life in the water, the beaver has a transparent eyelid, known as a nictitating membrane, that covers the eye when the beaver submerges. These waterproof "goggles" allow the beaver to see underwater without getting any irritating substance in its eyes.

The ears and nose of the beaver close tightly when the beaver dives. The ears are comparatively small and are located behind the eyes on the sides of the head. The nostrils are also on the sides of the nose, which allows them to be closed more readily underwater.

Water is prevented from going into the beaver's mouth by two folds of skin, one on either side of the mouth, that meet behind the front incisors. They effectively seal off the rest of the mouth and allow the beaver to chew on wood either on land or beneath the water, and yet get neither wood splinters nor water into its mouth.

The beaver's lungs have more oxygen capacity than do

human lungs. This means that with each breath it gets 50 percent more oxygen than we do. The beaver's blood system also helps it underwater. When submerged, less blood flows to the extremities — the forepaws and hindpaws — and more blood flows to the brain. The beaver's large liver also stores oxygen. All these factors allow the beaver to stay underwater for up to 15 minutes and to swim almost a half mile without coming up for air. However, most of the time a beaver will stay underwater for only 3 to 5 minutes.

There are five toes on each of the beaver's feet. Each toe has a stout nail. The two inside toenails on each back foot are split and are known as the "combing claws." They are used by the beaver in grooming its coat.

The front feet, from the end of the palm pad to the end of the longest nail, are 2½ to 3 inches in length. There are no webs or stiff hairs between the toes of the forefeet and they are as flexible as the human hand. These front feet are not used in swimming, but are carried balled up like fists against the chest.

The hind feet are strong and about 7 inches in length. The thin web of skin between each of the toes greatly increases the propulsion surface when the beaver swims.

Like birds, reptiles, amphibians, and many fishes, the beaver has only one body opening, called the *cloaca.* This serves as the genital tract for male and female organs of reproduction as well as for the excretion of body waste materials. The cloaca is located at the rear of the body under the tail.

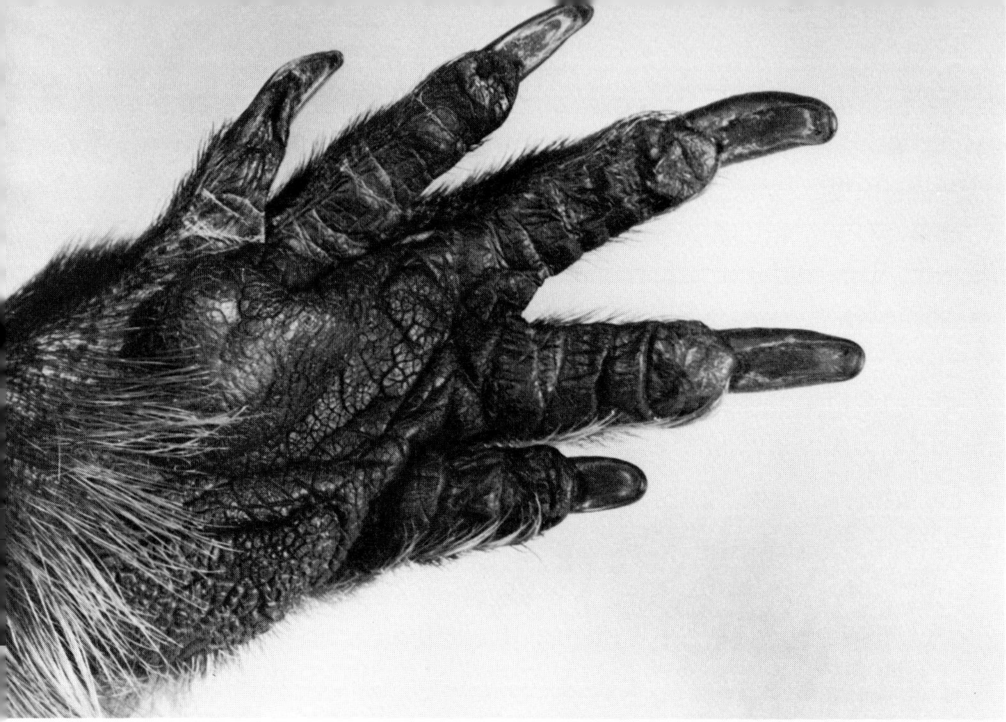

A beaver's forefoot

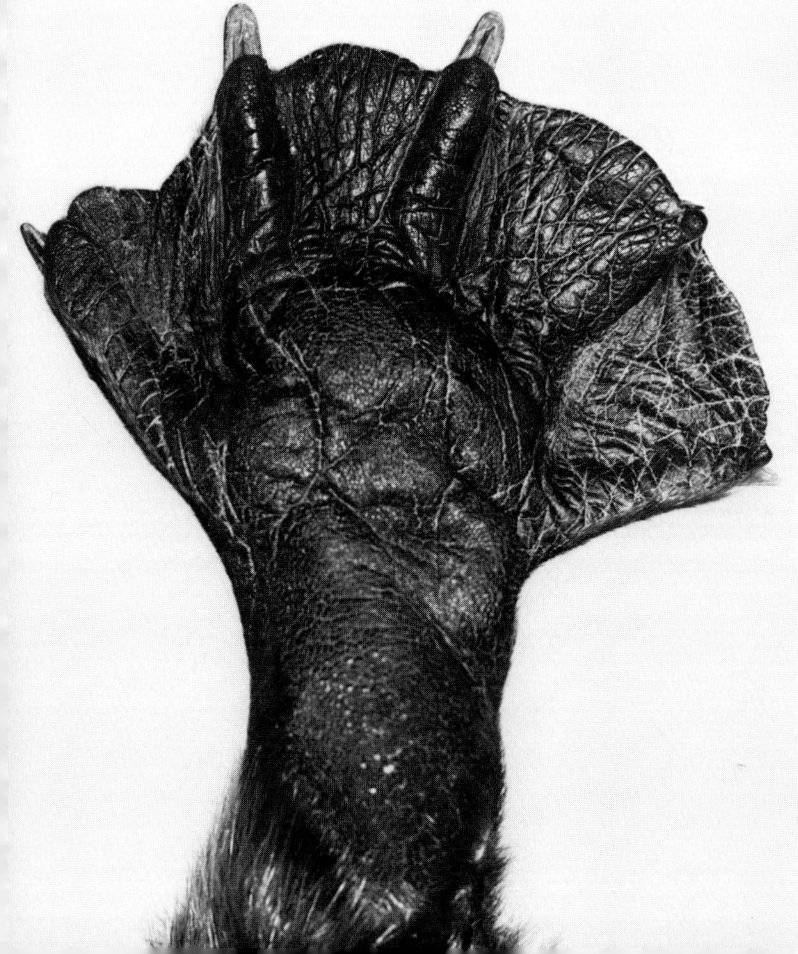

The right hind foot of a beaver

There are two sets of glands embedded in the walls of the cloaca. Two large castors, or scent glands, give off a thick, yellow oil with a strong, penetrating odor that is used for communication. This castoreum has long been used by humans in medicine, and it used to be considered a cure-all for such varied ailments as colic, rheumatism, arthritis, and pleurisy. The main use today is as a base for animal scents used in trapping. It is not only attractive to other beavers, but lures other animals as well.

To the rear of the castors are two smaller oil glands that are used for waterproofing the beaver's fur. The oil is rubbed on the guard hairs, which helps to trap air in among the fine undercoat. A healthy beaver, properly groomed, does not get its body wet when it dives beneath the surface of the water.

2

Where to Find Beavers

When the white man first came to North America, there were over 60 million beavers populating the area from what is now Alaska to the southern border of the United States. Most of the continent was home to the beaver. Every stream, pond, and lake that had available food supported its colony of beavers.

Scientifically, the beaver belongs to the mammalian order Rodentia, which includes all rodents. Its family name is Castoridae, its genus is *Castor.* At one time beavers were widespread in northern and central Europe where the animal was known as *Castor fiber.* In the New World the name is *Castor canadensis.*

The beaver is directly descended from the prehistoric Castoridae, which included beavers and other related rodent forms now extinct. The prehistoric beaver that roamed the eastern and southern United States during the Pleistocene epoch a million years ago was gigantic. It

A beaver on its dam

weighed between 700 and 800 pounds. Entire skeletons of Castoridae have been found in Indiana.

Beaver fur was so valued by Europeans that the early traders and colonists in North America found a ready market and all but wiped out most of the beavers to supply the demand. A fortune could be made in beaver pelts, and many were. The dark beaver fur was used for fur coats, but the fur was prized even more for beaver hats. By 1820 the last beaver was gone from New Jersey, and by 1865 from New Hampshire. Pennsylvania and New York were without beavers by 1890, and the situation was becoming much the same throughout most of the country. No laws protected beavers from year-round harvest until some states began passing them in the 1890s.

In the early 1900s, states without any beavers began to restock them from areas where they could still be found — Wisconsin, Wyoming, Minnesota, and Michigan. There are as many as twenty-five subspecies of the genus *Castor*, differing in size, color, and range. But today it is almost impossible to differentiate between them because of the crossbreeding done by man in efforts to repopulate them. There are now subspecies of beavers in ranges where they have never been found before.

By the 1920s, with the aid of bans on hunting and trapping beavers and man's efforts to restock areas where they had been exterminated, beavers have reestablished themselves successfully throughout much of the country. They are found today in most of their original ranges.

Beavers are regular stay-at-homes. However, each spring young beavers approaching their third year leave the colony to go off on their own before the mother gives birth to her young for that year. Research has shown that when the young beavers leave the area where they were born they are just as apt to go downstream as upstream. This is contrary to the general belief that the young beavers usually work their way upstream.

It has also been found that the young travel between

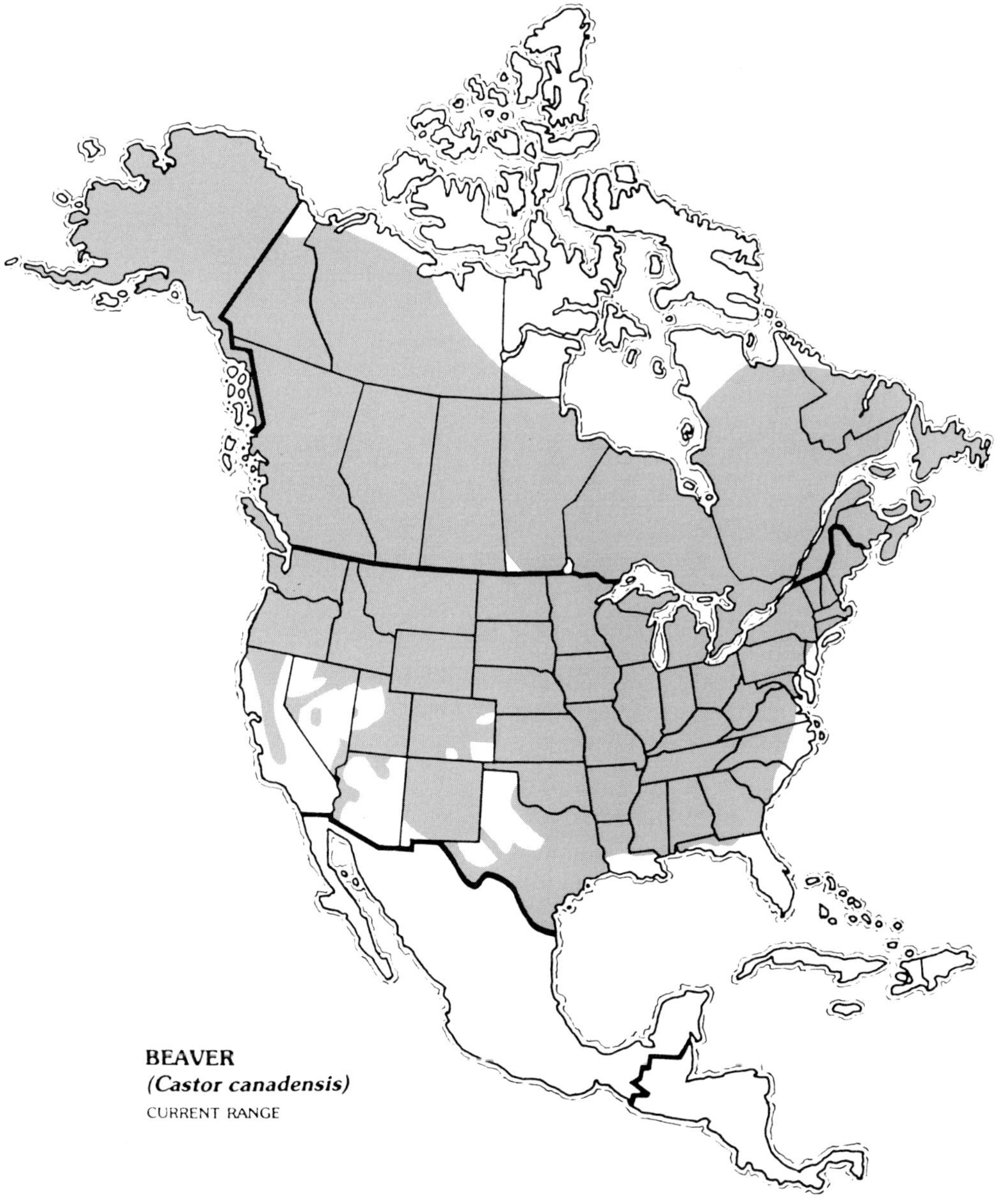

Distribution of beavers. Today they are found over almost all of their original range areas.

one and five miles before establishing a colony of their own. The travels of beavers have been recorded by "ear tagging." The distances they travel in a season, year, or lifetime vary. One two-year-old in Minnesota traveled 51 miles in one season; another two-year-old in North Dakota went 148 "stream miles" in seven months. That is not straight distance from the point of origin but actual distance the stream flows. Another tagged beaver traveled 135 miles over an eight-year period. These beavers are usually looking for new homes and mates.

3

Senses and Communication

The first thing a beaver usually does when it emerges from its lodge is to swim in circles with its head above water while its ears and nose search for the sound or scent of danger.

The beaver has a highly developed sense of hearing. Although the external portion of the ear is small, the auditory canal is large, and the beaver hears not only sounds on the surface but vibrations beneath the water. It can accurately classify them as being dangerous or not.

However, the sense of smell may be even more important to the beaver. Cutting and gnawing branches is a noisy business that blocks out other sounds. A beaver's vision is generally poor, although it can readily detect motion and the nictitating membrane over the eye allows it to see underwater. But a beaver depends on its sense of smell.

When a beaver is alarmed by some object that causes

A beaver sniffing for danger

it to be suspicious, it swims around that object until its nose can confirm its identity. Many times I have knelt in my canoe in the twilight hours studying beavers. Although I was motionless, I was in plain sight. When the beavers saw me they would not dive until they circled the canoe to pick up my scent. It seems to take the final confirmation of the nose for them to decide what action to take.

The taste buds of the beaver are well developed also. Beavers display definite taste preferences, preferring aspen and alders to pine, and they will not eat soured branches.

I led wilderness canoe trips in the north woods of Maine and Quebec for seventeen years. During that time I can remember many nights sitting with the campers listening to the sounds the beavers made. Beavers are extremely vocal. They talk to one another almost constantly. It is very easy to hear baby beavers whimper and whine inside the lodge. When the younger beavers ac-

Beaver babies accompany an adult to feed.

company the parents to feed outside the lodge, there is an incessant murmuring among all members of the family. They make a prolonged *ooooooooooooh* sound, rather like the noise a crowd makes on the Fourth of July after an especially beautiful starburst fireworks display.

A more strident note is a *yaaank,* which sounds to me very much like the call of a white-breasted nuthatch. An angry beaver hisses, much like the opossum.

The best-known sound of the beaver is its alarm signal made by forcefully slapping its tail on the surface of the water. This sharp crack, given on a quiet night, can be heard for a mile or more. It is a signal that is usually responded to by other beavers in the area. If you hear one slap, listen carefully. More may follow.

The beaver's scent post or pad is another means of communication. I have found that solitary beavers make and use these scent posts more frequently than do beavers in an established colony. Because of this, I feel that the scent posts are used more for advertising the presence of an unmated beaver than for a declaration of territory by an established colony.

These scent posts are simply piles of mud and grass and sometimes a few small twigs. They are perhaps 8 to 10 inches high and 10 to 12 inches in diameter. The mud on these posts or pads is usually kept fresh. After a post is completed, the beaver deposits its castoreum, from its castor glands, on the top. This musky-smelling oil is attractive not only to beavers but to other animals.

One can smell castoreum from long distances and I

The best-known sound of a beaver is its alarm signal made by slapping its tail on the surface of the water

have often worked my way upwind until I located the scent post. Imagine how far another animal, or the beaver itself, can detect castoreum. Probably a few drops of castoreum placed in water would travel many miles downstream to be detected by a beaver searching for a mate.

4

Beaver Locomotion

One of the first impressions I ever had of beavers was that they seem to do everything very deliberately, that they are cautious animals. On land they usually walk, and walk slowly, constantly stopping to sniff the air for potential dangers. When alarmed, they gallop — their fastest speed — but it is a gait that allows them to be outrun very easily by humans as well as other animals.

The beaver, at top speed, can run for a very short distance at about 21 miles an hour. A wildcat can spring at 50 miles per hour; wolves can run 35 mph. This makes the beaver very vulnerable when on land. That is why they are seldom found more than a few hundred feet from water and why they dig canals and escape tunnels filled with water. When they are in the water, it's another story.

Beavers had long been reported to swim at two miles per hour. Tests that I made showed that beavers usually

Underwater, a beaver uses only its hind feet for propulsion.

swim at 3 to 3½ miles per hour under ordinary conditions, but much faster when they want to. About 6 miles per hour is the beaver's top speed when it is swimming on the surface of the water.

When swimming, the beaver uses only its hind feet for propulsion. If it is swimming through brush, the forepaws are used to push aside the obstructions. When swimming underwater the forepaws are usually fully extended forward just before the beaver breaks through the surface in order to prevent collision with any object that may be floating on the water's surface.

When the beaver swims in leisurely fashion, it uses both its hind feet in unison. As the feet are brought forward, the toes are closed and curled to prevent drag. Then the toes and the webs are widely extended as the feet push back and propel the body forward.

If the beaver is alarmed or wants to get somewhere in a hurry, it will use an alternate stroking. I discovered this with the aid of a snorkel and aqualung, but today all you have to do is go to any zoo that has an underwater display window for a beaver colony and see for yourself.

The beaver's tail is used primarily for steering. It acts like a rudder. When a beaver is swimming at top speed underwater, the tail moves up and down, producing a sculling effect that increases the animal's speed.

A beaver entering its lodge underwater

5

What Do Beavers Eat?

If you were asked, "What do beavers eat?" chances are you would answer, "Trees." When I was young I had visions of hungry beavers devouring all the trees until there was nothing left. But beavers do not eat whole trees, nor do they eat the wood pulp. They have a varied diet.

The beaver's main food is the leaves, twigs, and the bark of trees that it fells. Generally the sticks used in beaver dams have first been used as food and are barkless.

Beavers eat 1½ to 2 pounds of food a day, which would amount to all the bark, leaves, and twigs on an aspen sapling 1½ inches in diameter. In spring beavers busily feed on skunk cabbage sprouts and roots, grasses, sedges, ferns, and water plants. Later in the season their diet includes twigs, leaves, fungi, berries, flags, spatterdock, water lilies, and duckweed.

Algae forming in warm water becomes an important midsummer food. It is high in protein. In the far north

Beaver feeding on algae

beavers often have to share this food with moose that also crave its nutritional value.

Near farms, beavers will eat wheat, oats, and especially corn. I made an interesting discovery some years ago near my home north of Blairstown, New Jersey. In an area where wood was scarce, a beaver had made a dam of cornstalks across a small stream. Beavers will also consume carrots, apples, potatoes, turnips, alfalfa, clover, and nuts.

In September the beaver's work increases furiously as it keeps foraging and begins to lay in its winter store of

A beaver feeding on a chip cut from a tree

A large beaver feeding on bark. Beavers eat bark, leaves, and twigs.

tree branches and saplings. They are felled by the hundreds and dragged beneath the water and anchored in the mud. I've watched beavers at this activity and was fascinated with the way they can drag a sapling underwater without just swimming in circles. While photographing them underwater I discovered that they use their tails as a compensating rudder that distributes the drag evenly.

One to two tons of food is necessary for the beaver family to survive the winter, depending on how many family members there are. This may seem like a lot of food, but it can be stored in an area 10 feet x 20 feet x 6 feet close to the lodge for easy access. Often the cache of food protrudes above the water.

The reason beavers wait until autumn to perform their food-gathering activity is so that the sap can return to the roots of the trees before they are cut down. This insures a minimum of spoilage. During the winter these branches are retrieved from the mud for food and eaten in the lodge. Only the bark is eaten, and beavers do this by rotating the branch in their forepaws, "corn-on-the-cob" style, leaving spiral teeth marks.

I have never witnessed a beaver catching and eating a fish, but there have been rare reports of this. It is entirely possible, since beavers swim as fast as some fish.

6

Birth and Young

A beaver family consists of the parents and the last two litters — a mother, father, yearlings, and the newborn young or kits. When young beavers get to be about 22 months old, they leave the lodge to go off on their own before the mother's kits for that year are born.

Breeding takes place in late January or February, depending on the area the beaver inhabits. Southern beavers naturally mate earlier than do those farther north. The gestation period is 107 days, or three and one-half months. This means that by May or June the female is ready to give birth.

Beavers are thought to be monogamous, having one mate until death takes one from the other. This does not seem so much a matter of choice as of conditions. The beaver's world at mating time is usually restricted to the pond where the lodge is located. Although the male may seek out additional females if given the choice — and

An adult and a yearling beaver

there are a few records of one male breeding with several females — icy conditions usually eliminate any choice.

Occasionally a small male may lose out to a larger male, but there is no evidence of beavers establishing the harems that some animals do. However, jealousy does exist among beavers. A strange male entering a colony will usually be attacked by the presiding male and strange females will be attacked by the adult resident female.

Most beavers are sexually mature by the time they leave or are driven from the parental colony at 22 months. In the far north some young beavers do not breed until their third year. Actual mating takes place in the water where the beaver's body weight can be supported.

Prior to the female giving birth, the dam is repaired and perhaps heightened. The male beaver and the yearlings usually leave the main lodge to set up temporary quarters in an auxiliary lodge or in a bank den.

The adult female then prepares the lodge for her young. She gathers birch and aspen sticks, cuts them to small

A beaver lodge and pond

A female during nursing season. Note the nipples.

lengths and carries them into the lodge. Using her incisor teeth, she splits them into long soft fibers. Grasses are not used for bedding because they would get wet while being brought underwater to the lodge and would mold and rot. The wood strips allow moisture to drain through and they remain soft and dry.

Beavers have only one litter a year and its average size is four, although three and five are common. One captive beaver in Salem, Oregon, had nine young. An overly large litter produces lots of friction because the female has only four nipples. One interesting fact is that the two lower nipples produce more milk than the top two. The size and weight of the mother determines the number of young in a litter. The largest females have the largest litters.

Several birthings of beavers in captivity have been witnessed and it is a process that may take 68 to 72 hours. That's three days! The baby beavers are born fully furred and with their eyes open. They weigh 13 to 16 ounces each and are about 12 to 15 inches long, including their tails. Their incisor teeth have appeared and within an hour they are nursing. The babies readily take to water without the usual urging that semiaquatic mammals must exert on their young. Some baby beavers have been seen swimming when they were only thirteen hours old.

When the baby beavers are two weeks old, they weigh about 1½ to 2 pounds. They will come out of the lodge to follow after the parents and to feed on whatever vegetation the older beavers are eating. At this stage, I have seen the mother beaver carry her young, horizontally in her mouth, like a dog retrieving a stick. She will do this when she wants them to be in a definite spot that perhaps they don't want to go to.

The newborn kits are especially vulnerable to attack by beaver enemies. Although otters, fishes, and owls are no match for adult beavers, they can easily kill a baby, and will if they have the opportunity. Some baby beavers have probably been gobbled up by the large great northern pike. Being a baby animal in the wild is very precarious, but it is nature's way of balancing itself.

An adult beaver with a yearling and three kits

The young are weaned — stop nursing — at about six to eight weeks, and go on the vegetarian diet that they will eat for the rest of their lives. The little beavers, unmolested, will grow to as much as 18 pounds by the end of one year.

The average beaver family will now usually consist of two adults, three or four yearlings, and three or four kits or babies. Males outnumber the females at birth, but by the time they are adults, there are more females. I have asked myself why, and can only suggest that perhaps the males are more venturesome and therefore more subject to predators. Whatever the case, it is yet another example of the balance of nature when left undisturbed.

It is difficult to tell the age of a beaver after about three years. They reach maturity at two years when they are capable of breeding. Based on a rule of thumb that the age at the beginning of breeding maturity is equal to 1/6 of a life span, the beaver can expect to live 12 years. However, beavers kept in captivity, protected from starvation, accident, disease, and natural enemies, live much longer. There is a record of a beaver caught in the wilds of West Virginia that was 21 years old.

The age of a beaver is probably more accurately told by its weight than by any other means. Beaver studies in Wyoming — the actual weighing of hundreds of beavers — produced the following age estimates. Kits weigh 9 to 15 pounds the first winter, yearlings weigh about 24 pounds, and adults weigh 40 pounds and up.

A male beaver with three young riding on its back

7

Beaver Behavior Through the Seasons

Spring

Spring is a time for the birth of the new kits. Adult beavers have bred in January or February, and every activity in the beaver colony during the following months becomes a preparation for the birth of the young.

[A beaver colony on a small stream can be one family. In more remote areas the colony may consist of a number of lodges, each with family units. Most lodges today have only one family. Many years ago, before the trapping pressure reduced their numbers, "apartment-type" lodges were a common feature. When I refer to a colony, though, I'm referring to a single family of beavers.]

Up to this time the family has consisted of the adult male and female, their offspring of two years ago, and last year's kits. Suddenly all this changes. Now the two-year-olds are driven forcibly from the lodge by the adults, if they have not left willingly. Rebuked and rebuffed,

A beaver forces a stick into its dam.

they know they are no longer wanted and set out on their own to establish a new family. This prevents overpopulation of the colony and prevents inbreeding of the species.

Before time for the birth of the new kits, the dam is repaired, in order to insure safe deep water around the lodge where the kits are to be born. The family, other than the mother, leaves the lodge for temporary quarters to allow the female to prepare the lodge for her newborn.

The baby beavers are soon out and about, with the mother looking after them. She feeds at night, and supplements their milk diet with various kinds of plant life. The kits are weaned within 5 to 6 weeks. By the time they are two weeks old, life returns to normal in the lodge as the yearlings and the adult male move back in and complete the family unit.

Spring is a time of comparative ease and relaxation for the beavers. The phrases "eager beaver" and "work like a beaver" do not apply to this animal during late spring and early summer, unless they are establishing a new colony. The main concern at this time is their daily food and caring for the young.

Their food is mainly grasses, ferns, roots, and water plants. They may cut down a few trees, but after being on a diet of bark all winter, they seem to prefer a little variety.

The young frolic about, playing tag in the water and generally scampering about, getting in the way. The adults keep a keen watch for predators that will find their defenseless young easy prey. The kits are subject to attack by foxes, martin hawks, owls, and even large fish.

When the evening's activity starts, it is the adult male that is first to leave the lodge. It is his job to scout the territory thoroughly before the young beavers go ashore to feed. The male usually swims in circles around the edge of the pond, testing the air for telltale signs of danger. Occasionally, a young beaver will become impatient and hurry up on the bank to feed. When this occurs, the large male will charge at the young one and perhaps even butt it with its head.

An interesting ritual to watch is the beaver's care and dressing of its fur immediately after leaving the water. It sits upright and carefully shakes the water out of its ears. It will then scratch its head, rub its eyes, and comb its whiskers. Then, stretching itself upright, it indulges in some good healthy belly scratching. Finally it begins to comb its fur, using the split toenails on the hind feet. I've timed them at this task for over five minutes. When all this is accomplished, the beaver oils its fur. To accomplish the oiling, the beaver sits on its tail by backing over it, exposing the cloaca where the oil glands are located. Reaching down with its forefeet, the beaver gets the oil and transfers it to its fur. This will take another five minutes, but at the completion its coat is waterproof.

A large beaver grooming

When the young beavers come out of the lodge they do not make too much disturbance because their small bodies do not displace too much water. They'll pop to the surface within a few feet of the lodge and swim back and forth. When the adults leave the lodge it is quite a thrill for the observer. They usually come out like a torpedo. There is a great disturbance of water and the surge offshore can cause enough turbulence to rock a canoe gently. Beavers usually void their body wastes as soon as they leave the lodge. They never soil the lodge itself and I have never seen their waste on land.

Summer

In areas where the beavers have complete protection, or at least are seldom molested, they will carry on their activities during part of the daylight hours. They will be most active in the late afternoon and the early morning, sleeping through the midday. The first explorers of North America wrote of how the beaver worked by day and slept by night. But the coming of the white trappers changed all that. To secure some measure of protection, beavers became nocturnal. Where disturbed, beavers carry on almost all their activities under cover of darkness.

The food of the beaver in summer depends on where it lives. It can be sedges, berries, wild roses, mushrooms, water lilies. If they are in a farming area, they'll eat anything the farmer grows. The main food, of course, is from trees that it fells.

When a beaver cuts down a tree, it has no control over

the direction in which the tree will fall. The beaver prefers to drop a tree into the water where it is more easily managed, and most trees growing near the water do just that because they get more sunlight on the side facing the water and the heavier limbs there cause it to fall in that direction.

When felling a tree, a beaver stands erect before it and braces its tail against the ground. Its forelegs either grasp the tree or rest against it. The beaver turns its head parallel to the ground and bites into the tree. Then, moving its head higher, it makes a second cut. It then grasps the piece of wood with its incisors and wrenches the chip loose. Then the entire procedure is repeated. As the beaver cuts farther into the center of the tree, the chips become smaller.

If the ground is level, the beaver may move around the tree as the cuts are made, so that the cuts are equally deep all the way around. If the tree is on an incline or the side of a hill, the beaver will make most of the cuts from the uphill side. It continues to cut until it hears or feels the last remaining fibers start to tear apart as the tree starts to fall. Then the beaver makes a dash for the safety of the pond. On rare occasions the tree may fall on the beaver, killing it, which only proves that the beaver did not control the direction of its fall.

Usually one beaver will fell a tree by itself. Occasionally, two beavers may work together, although I've never

When cutting down a tree, a beaver braces its tail against the ground.

Trees cut by beavers

witnessed this. When the tree is down, the beaver usually eats some of the leaves and twigs, and then the branches are cut off and hauled to the water. If the trunk of the tree is 6 inches or less in diameter, it may also be cut into pieces and rolled, dragged, or pushed into the water. I've seen a beaver push a log with its forehead or lie against it sideways and push with its shoulder. Beavers are exceedingly strong and can move logs weighing much more than they do.

In dense stands of trees, the beaver fells only four out of five trees it cuts. The trees often fall into and lodge in surrounding trees and do not come down. The beaver almost never cuts the supporting tree to make both trees fall, but I don't know why not. It seems to me that they are smart enough to figure out what must be done.

Beavers can cut down a ½-inch sapling in a single bite, and fell a 6-inch aspen in 10 to 20 minutes. There are records of trees 50 to 60 inches in diameter being felled by beavers. I have an end table in my home made from the stump of a beaver-cut tree that is 26 inches in diameter. I can tell that a large beaver cut that tree because of the size of the teeth marks. The larger the teeth, the larger the beaver. The incisors of a full-grown male beaver will be almost ⅜ of an inch in width.

Beavers are sociable while feeding and it's seldom that there is any fuss over food. The kits are especially favored in getting anything they desire, as the older beavers cut branches the kits can't reach. Adults often give up a branch they have cut for themselves. This friendliness is undoubtedly the result of beavers having little competition for food. Of all wild creatures, they probably suffer less from food shortage than any other.

The two-year-olds migrate in late spring and summer, searching for mates and new homes. As the young beavers travel about, they leave their "calling cards" in the form of mud patties saturated with their scent. All beavers make these, but the majority are the work of unmated beavers. If several young males locate a female at the same time, they probably will not fight over her. She chooses one, but I don't know what method she uses to make up her mind.

After a mate has been chosen, the pair will seek out a homesite. Most of their traveling will be done at night for greater protection. If they find an old lodge and dam that have been deserted because of a food shortage years before but has since regrown enough to support them, they may just move in and set up housekeeping. Whatever happens, they will search until they find ideal conditions for establishing a new colony. They spend two or three days checking things out before choosing an actual damsite.

Once a beaver decides where it is going to build its dam, that is where the dam will be built and nothing discourages it. Many times beavers could have done the same job with just a fraction of the work if it had only chosen a slightly different location.

Why do beavers build dams? Although the beaver is a large animal, it is not a fighter. It needs deep water in order to escape from its enemies. There is always more food growing along a small stream — in relation to the amount of water and the landmass — than there is along a large lake edge. So the beaver prefers to build a dam that will deepen the water in a small stream where there is lots of food. A beaver is easy prey to predators unless it has deep water in which to escape. The erection of

A beaver dam

just a two-foot dam will add enough to the stream depth to give ample protection.

A pair of beavers can build a dam two feet high by 10 feet across in a couple of nights. Never satisfied, the beavers will enlarge the dam as time goes on, but the small dam will suffice. They drag branches to the site and wedge them into place on the stream bottom, usually with the butt end upstream. The branches are weighted down with mud and rocks. Layer after layer is added.

A beaver carrying an aspen branch to the water

At first the dam is porous, which is as it should be so that the water pressure does not wash away the dam before enough mass and weight have been accumulated to hold it in place. When this has been accomplished, the beavers begin to pack the face of the dam with mud, leaves, and debris from the stream bottom.

Little by little the water level is raised and its weight

helps pack in the materials used on the face or upstream side. Dams are raised uniformly. Wherever a low spot develops, the beavers add more materials to make the height even. Dams are always much wider at the base than at the top. An average beaver dam will be 5 to 7 feet high and perhaps 75 feet long. However, many dams are 1,000 feet long or more, and the highest one I have seen was 10 feet high. The record for a beaver dam must go to one near the town of Berlin, New Hampshire. It was 4,000 feet long and created a lake containing 40 beaver lodges.

Spillways are often constructed as part of the dam or beside it in the bank to take care of excess water that fills up behind the dam. In time of floods the pressure on the dam may become so great that it will be washed out. The beaver will try to prevent this by cutting a spillway in the dam to relieve the pressure. I have seen this many times. After the flood waters have receded, the beavers have only to repair the hole they cut rather than replace the entire dam.

After a colony has become established, the beavers often build auxiliary dams both above and below the main dam. A dam below supplies back pressure which strengthens the dam, and one upstream takes pressure off. They also facilitate bringing in food more easily from a greater distance. It is much easier for a piece of wood to be floated and towed than to be dragged over dry land.

Occasionally families in adjoining colonies may help each other in repairs to a dam, but usually only one family

Beavers dig small canals to make the transportation of branches easier.

builds the dam originally. There are reports of adults helping inexperienced young beavers who are unable to complete a dam, but I have no proof that these stories are true.

Fall

Fall drives the beavers into a frenzy of activity as they build a lodge for protection against the coming cold weather. Even captive beavers will attempt to build a lodge when the days start to get shorter.

The beaver lodge is a marvel to behold, and there are many types of lodges. Bank burrows are usually dug at the same time the main dam is first constructed. These are temporary shelters, and will be used later as auxiliary shelters. Some beavers pile up wood on top of the earth of a bank burrow.

The ultimate in beaver construction is the "castle" type of lodge that is completely surrounded by water. To construct a lodge of this type, the beaver piles up logs, sticks, mud, and rocks in a mass on the bottom of the pond. The mass rises above water, usually 5 or 6 feet, and is perhaps 12 to 14 feet in diameter. I have seen beaver lodges that were 8 to 9 feet above water and 25 feet in diameter.

After the initial construction is completed, the beavers dive underwater and cut their way into the center of the mass. When they are above water level, they cut out a chamber 3 or 4 feet across and perhaps 18 to 24 inches high. Additional plunge holes or tunnels are also cut in. Each lodge has at least two entrances — most often more — for safety's sake. These will be straight tunnels to aid in carrying food into the lodge.

The chamber will have two levels. The first and main level is 3 to 5 inches above the water level and will be the feeding and drainage platform. After the beaver has entered the lodge by the underwater tunnel and drained most of the water from its fur, it then moves up to the bed area which is 8 to 10 inches higher. The bedding is made of finely shredded wood fibers.

The outside of the lodge is coated with liquid mud, except for the peak. The uncoated center section acts as an air duct or chimney. In cold weather the beaver's warm breath can be seen emerging from the lodge peak like

A beaver lodge with a good coating of mud

smoke. The mud-coated section of the lodge makes it waterproof and weather-tight. In winter it freezes to the hardness of concrete, preventing the beaver's enemies from digging through, if they reach the lodge over the ice.

A lodge varies in size with the beavers' needs and the length of time a beaver family has occupied it. In 1772, Samuel Hearne described a huge lodge in the Northeast from which Indians caught 37 beavers at one time. These "apartment-type" lodges were probably more common before constant pressure was put on the animals by the white man.

In 1809, John Colter escaped from Blackfoot Indians by diving into the water and hiding in a beaver lodge. Many years ago I tried to swim into a beaver lodge built on the headwaters of the Ottawa River in Canada. The lodge was 25 feet from the water's edge and a drought had exposed the tunnels leading to it. One of them was large enough for me — I thought. The tunnel was 22 inches in diameter and half-filled with water. After wriggling in about 18 feet, I ran out of head room and had to go completely underwater. I thought I could turn around, but while attempting a somersault, I got wedged upside down. I held my breath and wriggled myself upright and backed out of the pitch blackness. I've never tried such a stunt since and would not recommend it to anyone. I don't know what I would have done had I arrived at the lodge to be greeted by a family of angry beavers.

After preparing a home and repairing its dam, the beavers then turn to gathering a supply of food for the winter. Aspens are by far the most favored winter food, although the bark of white, red, and gray birches, maples, willows, alders, poplars, dogwood, beeches, and some oaks are also eaten in the northern United States. Pine hemlocks, balsam, cedars, spruce, and larches are cut and used for building but seldom for food. In the southern parts of the beaver's range the loblolly pine is the favored food.

When beavers begin to gather their food supply, they test the trees by biting into the bark to make sure the sap has run back to the roots. If there is too much sap in the trees, they may pass them by or speed up the drying process by girdling them. It is important that the bark be dry, because if it is stored underwater before it is ready, it will ferment and sour and be unfit to eat. The girdled trees are ready to cut in 5 to 7 days and are dropped at a tremendous rate. As the branches are chopped off, the beaver tows them back near the lodge and begins to make its underwater cache. Taking the branch in its teeth, the beaver dives to the bottom and forces the branch into the mud. More branches are added so that the additional weight on top prevents the bottom branches from moving. These piles are built as close to the lodge as possible so that they are easy to reach under the winter ice.

The beavers move farther and farther from the pond as they fell more and more trees. They'll dig canals a hundred feet long and 18 inches deep in areas where the land is level, to make transportation of branches easier. Where the land is steep, beavers will make pathways over which they drag branches. They will down trees on a hillside, but will not go over a ridge. It is too difficult to move cut branches or logs uphill.

One other job in preparation for winter is the digging of refuge holes at various spots around the pond wherever the bank is high enough to accommodate this. These will have underwater entrances with air channels above the water level. They give the beavers a spot to rest and breathe in when the pond is covered with ice. They also serve as a retreat in case the main lodge is broken into.

With all these precautions taken, the beavers are ready to simply wait it out as winter encases their world in snow and ice.

WINTER

Winter — at least in the northern part of their range — imprisons the beaver. Yet it is a lenient jailer that allows a great deal of leisure time and provides a greater measure of protection than any other season. The freezing weather that traps the beaver under the ice also turns the mud of their lodges into a hard consistency that is practically impossible for predators to destroy. Bears and wolverines may tear at a lodge, but usually are frustrated and leave hungry. The beavers are safe and snug inside.

The deep water around the lodge is very important to the beaver in winter. It allows them unrestricted passage

In winter the mud on a beaver lodge freezes as hard as concrete.

to their food supply. Although the water is cold, it never gets below freezing, or it would be ice instead of water. A proof that the beaver is relatively unaffected by the cold is the length of time it takes a beaver's pelt to become "prime" or fully developed. Land animals become prime in November or December, and beavers not until February or March. The beaver molts once a year, shedding its winter coat in late spring or summer.

When a beaver gets hungry in winter, it swims out to its food cache and brings back a branch to the lodge. Sitting on the feeding shelf, it cuts the branch into short lengths of about a foot to make handling easier. It will turn the stick with its forepaws, chewing off the bark with a "corn-on-the-cob" technique. When all the bark is eaten, the beaver will return the stick to the open water to float under the ice until spring. Then it may be retrieved and used to repair the lodge.

To supplement its winter diet of bark, the beaver will dig up the roots of whatever water plants are available. This is done close to the lodge and requires little air. Occasionally, if the beaver feels its lodge is being threatened, it may have to make an extended trip under the ice that requires more than one breath of air. Breathing under the ice is no great problem because the water level will often drop, allowing a pocket of air to form. If you walk across a frozen pond you can often see these air bubbles because the ice appears to be white where they are located.

A beaver carrying a large branch to the water

Beaver cutting up a tree branch

If a beaver cannot find an air pocket when it needs one, it can simply exhale the air in it lungs and follow that air bubble to the ice and rebreathe it. The filtering action of the water seems to remove some of the carbon dioxide and renew the oxygen. I have never seen a beaver do this, but I have seen muskrats doing it and I've no reason to doubt that beavers are able to do it. However, if a beaver is scared from its air bubble before it can breathe, it will drown. A beaver needs oxygen.

Breeding takes place during the winter months of January or February in the north, and the beavers begin the life cycle that will insure their continued existence. February is the trapping season, where allowed, and beavers are easy to trap. The trapper cuts a hole in the ice, baits his trap with fresh aspen sticks, secures the trap to a pole and thrusts the whole thing into the water. In trying to reach the fresh food, the beaver is caught and quickly drowns in the deep water.

Traps placed in shallow water where the beaver won't drown may cause the animal to lose a limb. Beavers have been known to live in apparently good condition with the loss of three of their legs, but this is cruel and no trapper should ever set a trap that does not immediately drown the catch. Traps should also be set a distance from the lodge so that the kits will not be caught, in order to ensure the survival of the species.

If the beaver escapes the dangers of the winter, as it has those of spring, summer, and fall, it is ready to begin the year anew.

8

Beaver Enemies

Humans have always been the greatest enemies of beavers — as hunters and trappers. Today, they are also competitors for habitat. Beavers are no longer hunted as they once were, but too often today we take more from the land than we replace, driving the wildlife into ever-shrinking areas and game refuges.

In the north country, the wolf is the beaver's principal enemy. While on land foraging for food, the beaver is exposed to attack by coyotes, lynxes, bobcats, mountain lions, wolverines, bears, and sometimes even stray dogs. However, a beaver is not an easy kill. Its weight is an advantage, its hide is tough, its body fat is a protection, and its powerful front teeth are formidable weapons of defense. Beavers fighting for their lives have been known to bite their attackers and drag them underwater to drown.

One aspect of beaver defense, or escape, is the beaver's use of plunge holes. These are made by the beaver digging long tunnels that are filled or partially filled with water.

A beaver is not an easy kill

One entrance is underwater and the other on land. Some are 30 to 40 feet from the shore and hidden by vegetation. If the beaver is cut off from the water by a predator, it will make for one of its plunge holes and disappear beneath the forest floor.

I have usually discovered these holes by inadvertently falling into them or falling through the roof of the tunnel. Most of the colonies of beavers I've photographed in Canada have these plunge holes, while most of those I've seen in the United States do not. The only explanation I have is that the Canadian colonies are mostly in virgin forest with the fallen trees of centuries making a running escape by the bulky beaver difficult. In the United States the colonies are in more open areas with less restrictive underbrush, making running to the water a better risk.

Once in the water, a beaver can usually make good its escape. It will dive beneath the surface and swim up to a half mile, usually to its lodge.

Beavers are subject to lice and mites and flies and mosquitoes. Flying insects can be avoided by returning to the lodge. Internal worms also plague beavers.

The disease tularemia at times wipes out the majority of an area's beaver population. It killed thousands of beavers in Ontario in 1949–51, and in Minnesota in 1951–52. This disease comes from a microorganism that lives in water. Those beavers living in running water are less susceptible to the disease because the microorganisms get flushed away. Animals living in still water suffer more from them.

9

Beavers and Humans

Most Indians in North America revered the beaver. All the northern tribes had legends about the "beaver people" and looked upon them as kind. The Crow Indians believed that when they died, they would come back to this earth in the form of a beaver. Therefore, each beaver was some relative or friend.

One tribe that did not hold the beavers in such high esteem was the Flatheads. They believed that beavers worked so hard because of sins they had committed when they were Indians. As a punishment, the Great Spirit changed them into beavers.

The Indians did hunt and trap the beaver for food and fur, but the small numbers they took did not make even a dent in the total beaver population. It was the Europeans coming to North America that changed the balance that had existed for thousands of years. They traded with the Indians for beaver fur, and trapped and hunted beavers all year round and wherever they were found. (Today, the trapping of beavers is limited, as we learn to conserve an animal that was very nearly obliterated from our landscape.)

Fortunes were made, wars were fought, and the continent was explored with the skin of the beaver often the driving force. The Dutch settled along the Hudson River, the English in New England, the French along the St. Lawrence River. Conflicts arose and wars were fought not so much for the territory as for the lucrative fur trade of each region.

The Hudson's Bay Company came into existence in 1670 for the express purpose of trading with the Indians for fur, especially beaver. Many other fur-trading com-

A beaver beside a large tree it has felled

panies were founded, and the heartland of the continent was opened up to exploration and trapping, with beaver fur too often the goal. Between 1853 and 1877, the Hudson's Bay Company alone traded in over three million beaver pelts. There are records of "mountain men" such as Alexander Ross trapping 155 beavers in one day and 5,000 in one season in the Bitterroot Mountains between the Columbia and Missouri rivers.

The reason beaver fur was so popular was not that beaver fur coats were so much in demand in Europe. In the late 1700s, beaver hats became the rage. These were not made from the skins. A special comb was used to pull out the soft underfur, leaving the guard hairs attached to the hide. It had been discovered that the beaver's underfur had microscopic barbs which allowed it to be pounded into a superior felt. This is what beaver hats were made of, and some of the best felt hats today are still made of this underfur.

Beaver pelts were sold by the pound. A large pelt weighed between one and two pounds, and the price was four dollars a pound. A 100-pound pack of 80 skins was worth three to five hundred dollars. An average trapline would yield a man at least sixteen dollars a day when most worked for 50 cents a day. Beaver pelts became the "money" of the wilderness. Guns and powder could be purchased with them, the value of a gun ranging from 8 to 14 pelts.

Beaver hats remained fashionable until about 1870. In 1832, a process to make silk hats was perfected and beaver hats began to go out of style. By this time, however, it was almost too late; most of the beavers had been eliminated.

A beaver going over the top of a dam

But not all of them. The beavers are back now and should be with us as long as we afford them suitable habitat. Many states have removed the beaver from the protected list in an effort to control their number and the damage they do.

When beavers move into a new area, nearly everything undergoes a radical change. Many of the smaller creatures, such as voles and shrews, will be flooded out and forced up to higher ground or out of the area entirely. Muskrats that may have lived along a fast-moving stream will move into the retained water of the pond formed by a beaver dam. Mink and otters will stay at the pond longer because the water now occupies a greater area. There will undoubtedly be many more fish. Moose and deer that were feeding on willows, alders, and maples on the banks of the stream will have to give up these trees as the beavers take them over. But there will be more water plants such as eelgrass and lilies. Many creatures will find the pond itself an obstacle to their travels over land, yet the dam will serve as a bridge over the stream.

As beavers continue to work and eat, they bring about many steps in plant succession. By felling trees around the pond, additional sunlight is allowed through and vegetation grows that might not otherwise. When the beavers leave, and before the dam begins to decay, the pond may silt up with rich topsoil or it may fill with soil that is acid and poor. If good topsoil, the result is a meadow and eventually the area returns to forest.

Index